Apr10- DPBG

LET'S PLAY SOCCER

Shane McFee

PowerKiDS press™

New York

Published in 2008 by The Rosen Publishing Group, Inc.
29 East 21st Street, New York, NY 10010

First Edition

Editors: Jennifer Way and Nicole Pristash
Book Design: Greg Tucker
Photo Researcher: Nicole Pristash

Photo Credits: Cover, pp. 5, 11, 15, 19 Shutterstock.com; p. 7 © AFP/Getty Images; p. 9 © www.iStockphoto.com/Thania Navarro; p. 13 © www.iStockphoto.com/Ana Abejon; p. 17 © www.iStockphoto.com/Dennys Bisogna; p. 21 © Getty Images.

Library of Congress Cataloging-in-Publication Data

McFee, Shane.
  Let's play soccer / Shane McFee. — 1st ed.
      p. cm. — (Let's get active)
  Includes index.
  ISBN 978-1-4042-4191-6 (lib. bdg.)
  1. Soccer—Juvenile literature. I. Title.
  GV943.25.M34 2008
  796.334—dc22

                                              2007029172

Manufactured in the United States of America

Contents

The Biggest Sport in the World

Soccer is one of the most popular sports for young people to play. People in countries other than the United States do not call the sport soccer, though. They call it football. In the United States, there is another sport called football. It would be hard to have two sports with the same name, so Americans call the game soccer.

Soccer is the most popular sport in the world. There are more than 240 million soccer players. Some of them are **professional** players and some play for fun. This book will tell you more about soccer and how you can join a team and start playing yourself.

Soccer can be played at home with your friends. You can also play on a team at school or in your town, like this player.

Two Thousand Years of Soccer

Soccer is over 2,000 years old! People believe that the first form of soccer was played in China in the year 300 B.C. A soccerlike sport was also played in the **Roman Empire**. These forms of soccer did not have the same rules the game has today. Soccer was not **organized** until several soccer clubs from England formed the Football Association, in 1867. The soccer played in England then is close to the sport that is played today.

The most important soccer games are played in a **tournament** called the World Cup. It is an **international** event that happens every four years. Almost every country in the world has a team in it with its very best players.

This is the crowd at a World Cup game between Germany and Argentina in 2006. Germany won with a score of 4 to 2.

Soccer Gear

The most important piece of soccer gear is a soccer ball. It is filled with air and weighs between 14 and 16 ounces (397–454 g).

Shin guards are also important. Shin guards tuck into your socks to keep your legs safe from kicks.

Soccer shoes are made for running and kicking. They often have cleats, or pegs, on the bottom. These pegs hold on to the ground as the player runs on the field.

Soccer players wear colorful uniforms so they can tell the teams apart. Soccer uniforms are special shorts that make it easy to run and special shirts called jerseys.

This player has all the gear he needs to play soccer. The cleats on his shoes help him change direction quickly when he runs.

9

The Team

Soccer is played on a rectangular field called a pitch. Both of the short ends of the pitch have a goal. The object of soccer is to kick the ball into the other team's goal.

Each team has 11 players. One player **defends** the goal. He is called the goalkeeper or goalie. The other players kick the ball around the field. Sometimes they hit the ball with their head and **torso**. Like many sports, soccer has referees to make sure both teams play fairly.

Soccer can be a hard game to play. Players must be very strong and be able to run for a long time. Soccer games last 90 minutes!

Goooooaaaal!

Soccer games have two periods that each last 45 minutes. During the game, the players try to score as many goals as they can, while keeping the other team from getting the ball and scoring goals. The goalie is the only person on the team who can touch the ball with his hands. If a player touches the ball with a hand or trips another player, the referee calls a **foul**. Fouls usually mean the **opposing** team gets a free kick.

The team with the most goals at the end of the second period is the winner. If the teams are tied, the game goes into overtime. This lasts until the tie is broken by making a goal.

Soccer players kick the ball very hard toward the goalie. Many goalies wear special gloves on their hands. Gloves help keep their fingers safe while catching the ball.

13

Kickers

Goalies guard the nets, but what do the other 10 players do? These players, or kickers, are called forwards, midfielders, and defenders. Their job is to move the ball up and down the field.

The forwards are also called strikers. They try to score goals. They must be fast. They must also be powerful kickers. The midfielders try to keep the ball away from the opposing team. They try to kick it to their own forwards. The defenders help the goalie defend, or keep goals from being made. Defenders try to kick the ball away from the opposing team's forwards.

There are generally two strikers playing on the field during a game. The other players try to pass the ball to them. Because of this, strikers score most of the goals!

Practice Makes Perfect

Soccer teams are led by a coach. The coach comes up with the **strategy**. A strategy is a system of plays that outsmart the other team. Soccer practice is where the team works on its strategy and skills. The most important soccer skills are dribbling, passing, and shooting.

Dribbling is running down the field with the ball. A good dribbler can keep the ball under control with her feet. Passing is kicking the ball to a player on your team. It takes good aim to keep the ball away from an opposing player while passing. Shooting is kicking the ball at the goal.

While a player is dribbling, someone from the other team will try to take the ball away. This is called a steal.

Teamwork

Playing soccer has many benefits. One important benefit is teamwork. Playing soccer helps you learn to work together with others. A good soccer player cannot be selfish. A good soccer player has to put the team first.

Soccer can also teach you sportsmanship. Sportsmanship means playing the best you can. Sportsmanship is also being a good loser and a good winner. After the game, the players on the losing team should always shake hands with the winners. Good winners do not brag or make fun of the losing team.

During a soccer game, this team needs to work together to make sure the other team does not score. They are practicing good teamwork.

Meet Freddy Adu

Freddy Adu is one of the best soccer players in the world. He is also one of the youngest.

Adu was born in the country of Ghana in Africa. He and his family moved to the United States when he was eight. Adu became the youngest **athlete** on an American sports team in 2004, when he began playing for the Major League Soccer team called DC United. He was only 14!

Adu is already a starting midfielder. He has appeared on two all-star teams. If he plays for a long time, he might become one of the greatest players in soccer history.

Freddy Adu started playing soccer when he was only two and a half years old. When he was 6, he played soccer with the older kids in his town.

Let's Get Active!

Does soccer sound like fun? Then you should play! The American Youth Soccer Organization can give you the chance to join a team with players your own age. Most towns and **regions** in the United States have teams in the American Youth Soccer League. The American Youth Soccer League will teach you how to dribble, pass, shoot, and other skills.

Someday you might go to a school that has a soccer team. Most high schools have them. You can also get together with a group of friends to practice and play soccer on your own.

Glossary

athlete (ATH-leet) Someone who takes part in sports.

defends (dih-FENDZ) Tries to keep the other team from scoring a point or a goal.

foul (FOWL) Breaking the rules of a sport or game.

international (in-tur-NA-shuh-nul) Having to do with more than one country.

opposing (uh-POHZ-ing) Being on the opposite side in a game.

organized (OR-guh-nyzd) Put things in order or made rules.

professional (pruh-FESH-nul) Someone who is paid for what he or she does.

regions (REE-junz) Areas.

Roman Empire (ROH-mun EM-py-ur) The powerful government based in Rome that ruled much of the ancient world.

strategy (STRA-tuh-jee) Planning and directing different plays in team sports or forces in the military.

torso (TOR-soh) The chest area.

tournament (TOR-nuh-ment) A group of games to decide the best team.

Index

Web Sites

Due to the changing nature of Internet links, PowerKids Press has developed an online list of Web sites related to the subject of this book. This site is updated regularly. Please use this link to access the list: www.powerkidslinks.com/lga/socc/

24